TENNESSEE

TWO HUNDRED

A

QUOTABLE HISTORY

OF THE

VOLUNTEER STATE

TENNESSEE TWO HUNDRED

A QUOTABLE HISTORY

OF THE VOLUNTEER STATE

BICENTENNIAL EDITION
ILLUSTRATED

COMPILED AND EDITED BY
RANDALL BEDWELL

GUILD BINDERY PRESS
NASHVILLE • MEMPHIS
1996

TENNESSEE TWO HUNDRED: A QUOTABLE HISTORY
OF THE VOLUNTEER STATE

Printed in the United States of America. Copyright
©1996 by Randall Bedwell.

Some quotes have been edited for clarity and brevity.

ISBN 1-55793-053-8

Library of Congress Cataloging-In-Publication Data
xxxxxxxxxx

Bedwell, Randall J.
Tennessee Two Hundred: A Quotable History of the
Volunteer State-- 1st ed.
        p.   cm.
        1. Tennessee history
        2. Regional/ Inspirational--Quotations, maxims, etc.

First printing
5   4   3   2   1

Guild Bindery Press books may be purchased at special discounts for fund-raising, educational or sales promotion use. Contact Guild Bindery Press, Inc. Post Office Box 38099, Memphis, Tennessee 38183.
Phone: 901.758.8577
E-mail: guildmedia@aol.com

Managing Editor: Robbin Brent
Senior Editor/Project Manager: Hollis Dodge
Contributing Editors: Palmer Jones, Robert Kerr, James Summerville
Layout and Design: Robbin Brent, RBrent&Company
Cover: Steve Diggs & Friends, Nashville, Tennessee
Photographs courtesy of Tennessee State Library and Archives.
Guild Bindery Press, Inc.
Post Office Box 38099
Germantown, Tennessee 38183

TENNESSEE TWO HUNDRED:
A QUOTABLE HISTORY OF THE VOLUNTEER STATE
BICENTENNIAL EDITION
ILLUSTRATED

INTRODUCTION BY GOVERNOR DON SUNDQUIST

Tennessee Two Hundred: A Quotable History of the Volunteer State is a splendid companion to our state's Bicentennial celebration. This is history vividly brought to life; a concise narrative of our state's settlement and growth that captures the spirit of the times through the stories and remarks of Tennesseans great and small.

Together they form a part of the tapestry of Tennessee, a part of the rich heritage we share and celebrate during our Bicentennial year 1996.

I hope that you enjoy this book as much as I have, and that the lively comments of our Tennessee forebears kindles both an interest in our state's heritage and an appreciation of the gifts others have lovingly passed down to us.

Governor Don Sundquist

$\mathscr{F}$rom slave narratives to the popular works of Studs Terkel, oral histories represent the substance of our national experience told by those who lived through it. First-person expressions are primary. They are the source materials from which interpretive histories are fashioned. Today, keeping pace with the past in a society transformed by sound bites, quotable history is simply oral history's latest, streamlined rendition.

With a minimum of added interpretation, this Bicentennial edition of *Tennessee Two Hundred: A Quotable History of the Volunteer State* represents the bold strokes of our past in the words of real Tennesseans. Mostly judicious, sometimes defiant, often sentimental, from Davy Crockett to Don Sundquist, their insightful words enrich us as they call forth an irrepressible appreciation of our heritage.

Randall Bedwell
Cordova, Tennessee
May 1, 1996

Settlement of Nashoba
Founded near Memphis in 1825 by reformer Francis Wright,
Nashoba's mission was to prepare slaves for freedom through
literacy and education

CONTENTS

Introduction

Chapter One
The People and the Land

Tennessee has a popluation that, in common, might vie with the populations in any country for all the best attributes of man.
James Fenimore Cooper, Notions of the Americans, 1828

$\mathcal{I}$n 1540 a Spanish expedition led by Hernando de Soto marked the first European penetration into the pristine Tennessee countryside between the Unaka Mountains and the Mississippi River. One thing was fixed uppermost in the Spaniards' minds: gold. When the only yellow metal they found turned out to be mere copper, the discovery of the Mississippi, or "Father of Waters," a short distance south of the Fourth Chickasaw Bluff, (near present-day Memphis), seemed little consolation.

While de Soto's party may not have realized that the true treasure was the rich diversity of the land itself, this fact was not lost on successive waves of English, Scotch-Irish, German and French settlers, who followed a century and a third later. Fearless and stout of heart, they crossed the mountains from the mid-Atlantic coastal states into the area that is now East Tennessee, which at the time was considered only an extension of North Carolina. The Tennessee River—that wild, winding, northward-flowing oddity, tamed only in this century—did not yet share its name with the land whose three Grand Divisions—West, Middle, and East—it designates.

The trio of circumscribed stars decorating the state flag attests to the geographic diversity of Tennessee, celebrated by country musicians and literary masters alike. Encompassing aged, craggy mountains and man-made lakes, tangled virgin forests and open meadows, undulating hills and furrowed bottomlands, each successive generation that comes of age in Tennessee shapes the landscape. And, in turn, they are altered by it in some way before moving on.

*I*f abused, they fight; if their rights are infringed, they rebel; if forced, they strike; and if their liberties are threatened, they murder. They eat meat and always their bread is hot.
John Trotwood Moore, historian, describing the characteristics of the Scotch-Irish people, forebears of many early Tennesseans

*T*ennesseans can go anywhere and do anything.
Aaron Burr, vice-president of the United States, 1800-1804

*T*he spirit of independence was the birthright of a majority of the District's settlers. Soldiers of the Revolution and their sons and daughters, soldiers of the Seminole War of 1812, of Jackson's campaigns against the Creeks, and against the British at New Orleans were leaders setting the tone and molding the sentiment in the new society.
Samuel Cole Williams, Tennessee Supreme Court Justice, characterizing early West Tennesseans

A man died and went to heaven. The celestial city was bright and glorious but there was one thing he didn't understand: People were tied to all the trees around. Finally, he decided he'd ask an angel who these people were. "Those folks are from Tennessee," the angel answered. "It's Friday, and we have to tie them up to keep them from going back home for the weekend."

A popular story in Northern cities during the industrial boom years, told by Tennesseans who had moved there for work

*T*he only difference between your home community and my home community is that Tennessee really is God's country.

Joe Clark, I Remember

I went alone that splendid morning through a country that I had not seen for a long time. All the bottoms were changed. Few patches of virgin woods remained. I know of no emotion that is at once so beautiful and pathetic as this sense of coming back after a lapse of time to roads one has walked in childhood.

Harry Harrison Kroll, novelist

The Smoky Mountains—it has a haze there that the other mountains don't have and it's real beautiful—very, very fine country.
Roy Acuff, country music pioneer

There is not a cranny in the rocks of the Great Smokies, not a foot of the wild glen, but harbors something lovable and rare.
Horace Kephart—author, outdoors scholar, "Dean of American Campers," and one of the founders of the Great Smoky Mountains National Park

This is mighty pretty country around here—the Great Smoky Mountains to the east and the Cumberland Mountains to the west. Don't blame my grandfather a bit for settling here.
William Gallaher, who patriotically and unquestioningly sold his land in 1942, when the government required property for the construction of the top-secret Oak Ridge, part of the atomic bomb project

Whether it proceeds from the goodness of the water, the purity of the air, the temperature of the climate or whatever else may have been the cause, the inhabitants of that country have certainly been remarkably healthy ever since they settled on the waters of [the] Cumberland River; whence it appears the climate is healthy and pleasant.
Gilbert Imlay, speaking of the inhabitants of Middle Tennessee, 1797

The plateau was comparatively level, though river and creek bottoms abounded; and at places far to the west might be seen an occasional near-mountain towering above the tallest trees of the forest and ribbed with rock—as if nature were again in sport. The soil was sandy and covered by a layer of leaf-mold, the deposit of centuries.
Samuel Cole Williams, describing early West Tennessee

It's the breath of life to me to go out into the woods, breathe the fresh air. Man's instinct is to be close to nature. We haven't been out of the woods that long!
Johnny Cash

*M*an is a child of Mother Earth and Father Time. His fullness of life requires that he have integral contact and conscious acquaintance with both parents. Strip him of his sense of place and his sense of the past, and he becomes inevitably unhappy.

Herman Clarence Nixon (1886-1967), professor of political science at Vanderbilt University and a contributor to the Agrarian manifesto
I'll Take My Stand

*I*f you're a boy and you have the choice between the eighth floor of a hotel and a big farm with horses, cows, canoes and a river, it was an easy choice for me.

Vice-President Albert Gore Jr.

David Crockett
(1786-1836)

A legendary
frontiersman,
Crockett
distinguished
himself in battles
against the Creek
Indians in 1814.
He served as a
Tennessee state
legislator and
U.S. congressman
before fighting for
Texas at the Battle of
the Alamo. Mexican
General Santa Anna
ordered his execution
on March 6, 1836

CHAPTER TWO
THE OLD ORDER:
COLONIAL ERA TO SECESSION

*The Union will be preserved, and treason and rebellion promptly
put down, when and where it may show its monster head.*
PRESIDENT ANDREW JACKSON DURING THE NULLIFICATION CRISIS,
OCTOBER 1832

*B*eyond the purview of established governments in
Virginia and North Carolina, the first settlers in East
Tennessee, William Bean and James Robertson among
them, faced down the crises of the frontier with practical,
precedent-setting solutions. In 1772, "by the consent of
every individual," the Watauga Association, which has been
called the "first independent government organized in
America," was formed to handle whatever official business
might require on-the-spot attention so far away from
proper legal channels. The association served as a model for

later settlements in the Cumberland Valley of Middle Tennessee, most notably at Nashborough (now known as Nashville, the state capital). Moreover, in 1784, citizens of the short-lived state of Franklin emulated the spirit of the Wataugans in their attempt to break away from North Carolina.

In 1790, the area that is now Tennessee was organized by the United States as the Southwest Territory. Although largely unsettled by whites, the new territory was far from uninhabited. In fact, it was widely populated by indigenous tribes of Cherokees, Chickasaws and other native peoples who had no conception of private property and had regarded the land as sacred hunting grounds for centuries (even reaching far back to ancestral memories of their predecessors, the mysterious mound-builders). Despite a vicious cycle of murderous raids and reprisals, men like Daniel Boone—respected "long hunters" who observed native ways — conducted negotiations with the Indians that enabled settlers to gain a foothold in the territory and eventually led to their complete control of the area.

Regrettably, the two cultures—Indian and White— fated to be on a collision course, never had an opportunity to reconcile. Tennessean Andrew Jackson, the first president elected from a frontier state, made it a top priority of his administration to forcibly remove the Indian tribes to Oklahoma. Ironically, in 1838 the Cherokee Trail of Tears wound its way directly past the Hermitage, Jackson's home just outside of Nashville.

In the early years of statehood, which came in 1796, politics in Tennessee had more to do with rivalries between strong personalities than ideological disputes. Territorial Governor William Blount along with William Cocke became the state's first U.S. senators. Indian fighter and Revolutionary War hero John Sevier was elected governor, and Andrew Jackson, then a young Nashville lawyer, became the first congressman. Sevier and Jackson were especially bitter enemies. Their political feud escalated into personal violence when Sevier insulted Jackson's beloved wife, Rachel, a divorcee, and a time and place were set for a duel. Fortunately, more words than shots were exchanged, and neither man was injured.

Despite his reputation as a product of his region, Jackson as president was a staunch and far-sighted defender of the Union. He regarded the Nullification Doctrine and its thinly-veiled secessionist threat as anathema.

While slavery was a question of central importance to

the country in the decades leading up to the Civil War, for many years the South's "peculiar institution" was forbidden as a topic of debate in the halls of Congress. Of course, this gag rule did nothing to prevent the issue from precipitating the costliest war in U.S. history in terms of human life. Tennessee was divided on slavery as few other states were; the Unionist counties of East Tennessee very nearly split the state in two, just as West Virginia split Virginia.

More controversy erupted in antebellum politics following the establishment of the Bank of the United States. Elected president in 1828, Jackson strongly opposed this institution and exercised his veto power to dismantle it. He defined his national political career through his outspoken views regarding the bank, which he saw as the insidious instrument of money interests maneuvering to loot the public purse through a disadvantageous debt-financed system. In fact, Jackson was the last president to operate the government with a balanced budget and pay off the national debt. Echoes of this 19th-century debate can still be heard behind today's headlines.

The manless land distinctly beckoned to the landless man.
Samuel Cole Williams

The Great Being Above is very good and provides for everybody. He gave us this land, but the white people seem to want to drive us from it.
Attakullakulla, civil chief of the Overhill Cherokees, 1772

You have bought a fair land, but there is a cloud hanging over it. You will find its settlement dark and bloody.
Dragging Canoe, Cherokee chief, to Richard Henderson, speculator, upon Henderson's purchase of 20 million acres comprising Tennessee land drained by the Cumberland River and all its tributaries—for 10,000 pounds worth of goods, 1775

I will sell them the land, but a few presents are as nothing compared to good land, which will last forever.
Chief Oconostota

$\mathcal{N}$o people are entitled to more land than they can cultivate. People will not sit still and starve for land when a neighboring nation has more than it needs.
Judge David Campbell, 1782

$\mathcal{T}$ruth is, if we had no land, we should have fewer enemies.
Old Tassel, Cherokee leader, 1782

William Blount (1749-1800)
In 1790, Blount, a native of North Carolina and avid land speculator, became governor of the Southwest Territory, as Tennessee was known before it was granted statehood. Along with William Cocke, Blount served as one of Tennessee's first U.S. senators.

*T*have a pipe and a little tobacco to give the commissioners to smoke in friendship. I am now old, but hope yet to bear children who will grow up and people our nation, as we are now under the protection of Congress and have no more disturbances.

Nancy Ward, acting as spokesperson for the Cherokee nation, 1785. Nearly a decade before, Ward had saved Mrs. William Bean from being burned at the stake by warriors of her tribe

*T*he Cherokees, I believe, sincerely wish peace, but the Creeks must be humbled before you can enjoy peace, and I fear that wished-for period will never arrive until this [Southwest] Territory becomes a state and is represented in Congress.

William Blount, territorial governor, 1794

*I*f I have erred, I shall ever regret it.

James Robertson, sometimes called "the Father of Tennessee," on being forced to resign his military commission after defying federal orders prohibiting all but defensive use of troops against the Indians. With the tacit approval of Gov. Blount, Robertson led the notorious Nickajack Expedition in 1794, during which a number of Chickamauga villages were burned to the ground

*T*he appointment is truly important to me. My Western lands had become so great an object to me that I should go to the Western Country to secure them and perhaps my presence might have enhanced their value. I am sure my present appointment will.

William Blount upon receiving his appointment as territorial governor of the Southwest Territory [Tennessee] from President George Washington. Characteristically, land speculation was uppermost in Blount's mind

*W*hen I reflect that not one in a hundred come here to get religion, but rather to get plenty of good land, I think it will be well if some or many do not eventually lose their souls.
Francis Asbury, Methodist bishop

*W*e the People of the Territory of the United States south of the river Ohio ... do ordain and establish the following constitution, or form of government—and do mutually agree with each other to form ourselves into a free and independent state, by the name of THE STATE OF TENNESSEE.
excerpt from the preamble to the 1796 Constitution, read amid cheers at the first Constitutional Convention, February 6, 1796

John Overton (1766-1833)
A judge, land speculator, frontier businessman and friend and ally of Andrew Jackson. Overton counted the fourth Chickasaw Bluff overlooking the Mississippi River among his holdings. The city of Memphis was eventually founded on the site. His partners in the venture were Andrew Jackson and James Winchester. Thanks to Overton's efforts, Memphis became an important river town

A poor pitiful petty fogging lawyer.
Gov. John Sevier's opinion of political rival Andrew Jackson. Sevier blocked Jackson's first attempt to become major general of the Tennessee militia in 1796

I must beg leave to congratulate you on your interest and popularity in this country. Your election is certain and I believe that there is scarcely a man in this part of the territory that could be elected before you.
John Overton to Andrew Jackson, on the latter's election, at age 29, to the House of Representatives, 1796

I know of no great service you have rendered the country, except taking a trip to Natchez with another man's wife.
John Sevier to Andrew Jackson, October 1, 1803

$\mathcal{D}$id you take the name of a lady into your polluted lips in the town of Knoxville? Did you challenge me to draw, when you were armed with a cutlass and I with a cane, and now, sir, in the neighborhood of Knoxville you shall atone for it or I will publish you as a coward and a poultroon. ... I shall expect an answer in the space of one hour.

Andrew Jackson to John Sevier, issuing a challenge to a duel, October 3, 1803

$\mathcal{I}$ am of the opinion that a good judiciary lends much to the dignity of a state and the happiness of the people. On the contrary a bad judiciary involved in party business is the greatest curse that can befall a country.

Andrew Jackson to William Blount

Well, Colonel, I suppose we shall have a radical change of the judiciary at the next session of the legislature. 'Very likely, sir,' says I, and put out quick, for I was afraid someone would ask me what the judiciary was and if I knowed I wish I may be shot. I don't believe I ever heard there was any such thing in nature, but still I was not willing that the people there should know how ignorant I was about it.
Davy Crockett as a freshman member of the Tennessee General Assembly, quoted from his autobiography

Look at my neck and you will not find any collar with the label: "My Dog, Andrew Jackson."
Davy Crockett, on his political independence from Andrew Jackson

I would sooner be honestly and politically damned than hypocritically immortalized.
Davy Crockett

You can go to Hell. I'm going to Texas.
Davy Crockett to his constituents, after being defeated for re-election to the House by Jackson-backed candidate Adam Huntsman, 1834. Crockett had voted against Indian removal

GTT
initials found carved or painted on a number of abandoned dwellings in Tennessee in the late 1820s and 1830s. The letters stand for "Gone to Texas"

It is said abroad that the common people would gladly remove, but are deterred by the chiefs and a few other influential men. It is not so I say with the utmost assurance, it is not so. The whole tide of national feeling sets in one strong and unbroken current against removal to the west [to Oklahoma].
"Cherokee Messenger" Samuel Austin Worcester, the missionary, teacher and early printer and publisher for the Cherokees utilizing Sequoyah's alphabet

James Robertson (1742-1814)
In 1779, Robertson led a small party of settlers from East
Tennessee to the site of present-day Nashville. For this feat,
among others, he is considered "the Father of Tennessee"

When a people has their heads in the Lion's mouth, prudence requires them to take it out with great care. We are all laboring in great suspense to hear our final doom.
Cherokee Chief John Ross on the eve of the forced removal of his people from Georgia, North Carolina and Tennessee along the Trail of Tears to Oklahoma

The politician who will be useful in the United States must permit his mind to comprehend the various interests of the different sections of the country. He who will not permit his mind so far to expand as to embrace the whole extent of his own country will always be in danger of inflicting injury, while he intends to afford protection.
Hugh Lawson White, Tennessee Supreme Court justice and U.S. Senator

It is to be regretted that the rich and powerful too often bend the acts of government to their selfish purposes.
President Andrew Jackson vetoing the recharter of the Bank of the United States, July 10, 1832

It is a daring enterprise in any light in which it can be viewed, in any man, to attempt to wear the armor of the political Achilles! It is no puny arm that can wield the truncheon of Jackson.

John Bell, on Jackson's supposed intent to install a presidential successor of his own choosing, 1835

In all probability the attempt to place me in the first position [on the Democratic ticket] would be utterly abortive.

James K. Polk to Andrew Jackson, responding to Jackson's insistence that Polk run for president, 1844

In the confusion that will prevail, there is no telling what may occur.

James K. Polk speculating about the Democratic Convention in Baltimore, 1844

They can use my name in any way they may think proper.

James K. Polk, 1844. The Democrats nominated Polk on the ninth ballot over Martin Van Buren and others

I intend to be myself president of the United States.
James K. Polk to Congressman Cave Johnson, 1844. Polk won the election but failed to carry Tennessee. He lost his home state to Whig candidate Henry Clay by less than 100 votes

I wish to Almighty God that the whole American people could be assembled in this city [Washington, D.C.] and the veil that now conceals from their view the many abuses could be drawn aside, and they be permitted to take one calm survey, one full and dispassionate view, of all the secret springs of the entire proceedings of things under this Government, of all the intriguings of officers in authority from the highest to the lowest.
Congressman Andrew Johnson attacking President Polk's administration, 1847

It will be readily perceived by all discerning young men that Democracy is a ladder, corresponding in politics to the one spiritual which Jacob saw in his vision; one in which all, in proportion to their merit, may ascend. While it extends to the humblest of all created beings on earth, it reaches to God on high.
Governor Andrew Johnson, inaugural address, 1853

*W*hat! Pray for the salvation of Andrew Johnson! Why, to save him would exhaust the plan of Salvation, and where would the rest of us be?

Meredith P. Gentry responding to W.G. "Parson" Brownlow, after losing the 1855 gubernatorial race to Johnson. Brownlow urged Gentry to pray for Johnson rather than curse him

*S*lavery is unfriendly to a genuine course of agriculture, turning in most cases the fair and fertile face of nature into barren sterility. It is the bane of manufacturing enterprise and internal improvements; injurious to mechanical prosperity; oppressive and degrading to the poor and laboring classes of the white population that live in its vicinity; the death of religion; and finally it is a volcano in disguise, and dangerous to the safety and happiness of any government on earth when it is tolerated.

Thomas Roan speaking before the Tennessee Manumission Society, 1820

*L*ive the Union; perish slavery.
Judge Oliver Perry Temple (1820-1907) canvassing against secession in East Tennessee, 1861

*S*how me the man who has been engaged in these conspiracies, who has fired upon our flag, who has given instructions to take our forts and custom houses, our arsenals and dockyards, and I will show you a traitor.
Senator Andrew Johnson, March 3, 1861. Johnson denounced the Southern secessionists in a famous speech on the very last day of the 36th Congress. It was said that after Johnson delivered the speech, he became "the most popular man in the North, excepting Lincoln"

Andrew Jackson (1767-1845)
A gifted soldier, jurist and duelist, Jackson was the first chief
executive elected from a frontier state. During his administration, the national debt was paid off in 1835, and the surplus
revenue was distributed among the states

CHAPTER THREE
FILLING THE MUSTER ROLLS

---

*Tennessee will not furnish a single man for purposes of coercion,
but 50,000 if necessary for the defense of our rights and those of
our Southern brothers.*
GOVERNOR ISHAM G. HARRIS' RESPONSE TO PRESIDENT LINCOLN'S CALL
FOR TROOPS AFTER FORT SUMTER, 1861

*D*uring the battle of Okinawa near the end of the
Second World War, Japanese banzais were reported
to have yelled as their war cry, "To hell with President
Roosevelt, to hell with Babe Ruth, to hell with Roy
Acuff!" While the legendary fighting prowess of wartime
Tennesseans such as the famed "Old Hickory" Division,
has been enhanced with each successive conflict our
nation has entered, the state's martial reputation rests forever on the wars of the last century.

Great empires go to war during their rise and decline, rarely at their apex. In his revolutionary treatise On War, Karl von Clausewitz wrote "War is a continuation of politics by other means." In the ascendant years of the American Republic, diplomatic breakdowns were a frequent occurrence, and the brash young country never hesitated to settle its disputes on the battlefield. The military successes of the era were due in large measure to the fighting skill and enthusiasm of Southerners, especially Tennesseans.

Surprisingly, as relations between the American colonies and Britain soured, leaders of the Southern provinces were the most conciliatory toward the crown and reluctant to declare themselves in open revolt. The true fomenters of rebellion were Northeastern firebrands like Samuel Adams, and, indeed, when the Revolution first broke out in armed conflict, it was at Lexington and Concord, not in Virginia. Once blood had been spilled, however, Southerners stepped valiantly into the fray.

In the critical year of 1780, the Overmountain men, a militia of East Tennessee frontier troops commanded by John Sevier and Isaac Shelby, met and repulsed a British force at King's Mountain, just across the South Carolina line. Considered the turning point of the war in the South, the British loss at King's Mountain convinced the "redcoats" to abandon North Carolina and move farther north. Just over a year later, on October 19, 1781, General Cornwallis' army would surrender at Yorktown, Virginia.

Despite the American victory in the War of Independence, Britain and her breakaway colonies continued to wrangle over issues such as the impressment of American sailors into the Royal Navy and England's anti-American agitation among the Indian tribes, especially the Creeks. Within a quarter century, hostilities once again came to a head. Known popularly as the War of 1812, the conflict's decisive battle was fought on January 8, 1815, at New Orleans. There, General Andrew Jackson (dubbed "Old Hickory" by his troops) led a force consisting largely of his fellow Tennesseans and their Indian allies against the superior numbers of the British Army under Maj. General Sir Edward Packenham. Unbeknownst to either commander, however, the warring nations had concluded a peace treaty on Christmas Eve, rendering a military solution unnecessary. Nevertheless, fighting commenced and Jackson's army won an overwhelming triumph with almost no American lives lost. The victory was an incredible boon for the prestige of the United States abroad and started Andrew Jackson on the road to the White House.

Rooted in the martial traditions of Tennessee, one surviving legacy of the War of 1812 is the nickname "Volunteer State." Acting without federal authorization, the Tennessee General Assembly called for 3,500 troops to fight the British. The response from volunteer recruits was overwhelming and the quota could have been met many times over. In fact, a similar scenario developed three and a half decades later when, in 1846, the United States went to war with Mexico. This time Washington requested only 2,800 soldiers, but 30,000 Tennesseans clamored to join—some even offering to pay for the privilege. With Tennessean James K. Polk (known as "Young Hickory" to both his Democratic supporters and Whig opponents) sitting in the White House and many former Tennesseans, such as Sam Houston, "gone to Texas" (the state most in harm's way), Tennessee had a vested interest in seeing the war brought to a successful conclusion.

In a few short years, Tennessee itself would become the battleground. As a border state during the War Between the States, Tennessee was the unfortunate front along which much of the fighting in the west occurred. From Fort Donelson to Shiloh, Chickamauga to Franklin, no state, save Virginia, saw more blood shed on its soil. Indeed, the Battle of Shiloh became the largest land battle ever fought in North America at the time. Appropriately, the two opposing Union and Confederate armies locked in that struggle both used the state's name as part of their appellation, calling themselves the Army of Tennessee (CSA) and the Army of the Tennessee (USA).

Tennessee's role in the Civil War was schizophrenic as well as bloody, as the state found its loyalties pulled in opposite directions. Although the government in Nashville was Confederate and roughly 100,000 Tennesseans served in the Confederate army, about 50,000 joined the Union ranks. In fact, Tennessee provided more soldiers for the Union cause than any other Confederate state. In addition, more Confederate soldiers came from Tennessee than almost any other state. Not surprisingly, such deep divisions required decades of heal·ing before the bitterness caused by the war subsided.

John Sevier (1745-1815)
Sevier became Tennessee's first governor in 1796 and served five more terms in that office. He later served terms in the Tennessee Senate as well as the U.S. Congress until his death.

Here, Mr. Sevier, is another of your boys [James] who wants to go with his father and brother Joseph to the war; but we have no horse for him, and, poor fellow, it is too great a distance for him to walk.

Bonny Kate Sevier to her husband John. James Sevier, only 15 at the time, was her stepson. Prelude to King's Mountain, 1780

When we encounter the enemy, don't wait for the word of command. Let each one of you be your own officer.

Col. Isaac Shelby to his men, Battle of King's Mountain, 1780

I remember well the deep and grateful impression made on the mind of every one by that memorable victory. It was the joyful annunciation of that turn of the tide of success which terminated the Revolutionary War with the seal of our independence.

Thomas Jefferson, on the Battle of King's Mountain, 1780

*U*nited and firm, let us obey the call of our Country and be prepared to fight at nought the machinations of those sanguinary bands of hirelings when they shall dare assail our rights or liberties.

Meriwether Lewis supporting President Thomas Jefferson's call for 100,000 militiamen in 1808 when relations with Britain grew strained. When war broke out in 1812, the overwhelming response of Tennesseans to arms earned Tennessee the nickname "Volunteer State"

I firmly believe that Great Britain must recede or this Congress will declare war. If the latter takes place, Canada and the Floridas will be the theatres of our offensive operations.

Congressman Felix Grundy to Andrew Jackson. Grundy was known as one of the War Hawks who urged war with Great Britain in 1812

Andrew Johnson (1808-1875)

As leader of the Southern Union men, Johnson opposed the forces of secession in Tennessee during the Civil War. He was military governor of his conquered home state before Lincoln chose him as his vice-presidential running mate in 1864

I had rather all my sons should fill one honorable grave, than that one of them should turn his back to save his life. Go, and remember, too, that while the door of my cottage is open to brave men, it is eternally shut against cowards.
Sam Houston's mother, spoken to Houston as he departed Blount County for the War of 1812

B efore they [the British] reached our small arms, our grape and canister mowed down whole columns, but that was nothing to the carnage of our rifles and muskets.
General John Coffee describing the Battle of New Orleans, 1815

T he cup of forbearance has been exhausted. ... Mexico has passed the boundary of the United States, has invaded our territory and shed American blood upon American soil. She has proclaimed that hostilities have commenced, and that the two nations are now at war.
President James K. Polk, in his message to Congress asking for a declaration of war, May 12, 1846

*N*o matter what your country's cause or quarrel, it is enough for the patriot to know she is in a war. Be her cause right or wrong, it is your duty to espouse it, and if she calls on you to command her armies, to lead them to victory or death.

Gideon Pillow, in an address at the University of Nashville, 1856. Pillow would later become commander of the Confederate Army of Tennessee

*H*ere's to the lads of Tennessee
      The bravest in the land;
One half wolf, one half hoss
      and the other half, just man.
           —Civil War song

*I*did not come here for the purpose of surrendering my command.

Nathan Bedford Forrest, Fort Donelson, 1862

Albert Sidney Johnston surprised General Ulysses Grant by
attacking the Union Army at Shiloh, April 6, 1862. Pressing
his advantage, Johnston was mortally wounded in the afternoon
of the first day of battle. He died from loss of blood.
A simple tourniquet could have saved his life

We shall attack at daylight tomorrow. I would fight them if they were a million.
Gen. Albert Sidney Johnston, Shiloh, 1862

Tonight we will water our horses in the Tennessee River.
Gen. Albert Sidney Johnston, Shiloh, 1862. Johnston, who at the time was considered the South's greatest soldier, was killed on the afternoon of the first day of battle

The battle is lost.
Gen. Braxton Bragg, upon receiving Gen. Beauregard's order to cease fighting, Shiloh, April 6, 1862

*I*n my justifiable attacks on Federal Troops and Federal property, I have always respected private property and persons of Union men. I do hereby declare that, to protect Southern citizens and their rights, I will henceforth put the law of retaliation into full force, and act upon it with vigor. For every dollar extracted from my fellow citizens, I will have two from all men of known Union sentiments, and will make their persons and property responsible for its payment.

John Hunt Morgan, the "Rebel Raider," 1863

Isham G. Harris (1818-1897)

As governor, Harris was instrumental in carrying Tennessee out of the Union. In February 1861, Tennesseans voted down a proposal to call a convention that would take up the question of secession. Harris and his secessionist cohorts then manipulated the situation and created an independent Tennessee, neither Union nor Confederate. From this isolated position, subsequent military developments would push Tennessee into the Confederate fold

*G*et there first with the most men.
famous maxim of Gen. Nathan Bedford Forrest

I killed a good many men, of course. I don't deny that, but never killed a man who was not seeking my life. ... I don't know some of the things in these specifications, but I don't deny anything I ever done. I want to be sent to my family. I don't want to be buried in this soil.
last words of Champ Ferguson, White County native and Confederate "bushwhacker," before his execution in Nashville

If you surrender, you shall be treated as prisoners of war, but if I have to storm your works, you may expect no quarter.
General Nathan Bedford Forrest's infamous ultimatum to Union soldiers, many of whom were black, before the Ft. Pillow capture, 1864

*W*ar means fighting, and fighting means killing.
General Nathan Bedford Forrest

*A*ny man who is in favor of a further prosecution of this war is a fit subject for a lunatic asylum, and ought to be sent there immediately.
General Nathan Bedford Forrest

A man I have never seen, sir. His name is Forrest.
Robert E. Lee's response when asked who was the greatest soldier under his command, Appomattox, 1865

*W*ell, if we are to die, let us die like men.
last reported words of General Pat Cleburne, Franklin, 1864

*D*amn the torpedoes—full speed ahead!
Admiral David G. Farragut, Battle of Mobile Bay, August 5, 1864

Matthew Fontaine Maury (1806-1873)
An eminent oceanographer, Maury was a leading figure in the
Confederate Navy and, after the war, was instrumental to the
Trans-Atlantic cable project, which established immediate
communication (via the telegraph) between
Europe and America

Chapter Four
March of Progress:
Reconstruction to Bicentennial

This is as brazen and bold an attempt to destroy liberty as was ever seen in the Middle Ages. ... Not a single line of any constitution can withstand bigotry and ignorance when it seeks to destroy the rights of the individual.

Clarence Darrow, Scopes' lawyer for the "Monkey" Trial, 1925

*T*ennessee was the last state to leave the Union and the first to return. If any one factor set the state apart from the rest of her Confederate allies and determined her future in the post-bellum era it is this often noted circumstance. With much of the state under federal control after 1862, Reconstruction arrived earlier here than in other areas of the South. As a result, Tennessee was readmitted to the Union in 1865, the year the war ended, and the third Tennessean in less than four decades became president.

On Lincoln's assassination—the signal event that sparked national chaos in the war's aftermath—Vice-President Andrew Johnson, a pre-war Democrat, became the nation's 17th chief executive. An auto-didactic tailor from Greenville, Johnson had been a leading Southern Unionist and, as military governor, architect of the state's accelerated Reconstruction. Earning a reputation during the war as a hard-liner who favored punitive measures against former Confederates, Johnson as president stunned the country when, in the spirit of his predecessor, he adopted a more conciliatory attitude toward those lately engaged in hostilities. Johnson's policy placed him in irreconcilable opposition to a Congress dominated by Radical Republicans, who favored maintaining martial law throughout the South. A crisis between the two branches of government ensued when Johnson violated the dubious Tenure of Office Act by removing war secretary Edwin M. Stanton without Senate consent. Ostensibly, it was for this offense that Johnson was impeached. However, the underlying cause, evident to many at the time and more after Johnson's acquittal, was the dispute over competing plans for Reconstruction.

Johnson's about-face on Reconstruction, which presumably brought about his impeachment in Washington, did not play well at home either among the Unionists who now controlled Tennessee. Like John Quincy Adams before him, Johnson sought to return to Congress after serving out his term as president. His only problem was getting elected. The former president suffered losses in three elections—one for the Senate, two for the House—before being returned briefly to the Senate in 1875. He died in July of that year.

A longtime Johnson antagonist who plagued the president throughout his career, despite their shared Unionist loyalties, was William G. "Parson" Brownlow, a Methodist circuit rider who gave up the pulpit for politics. During the war, the two temporarily put aside their differences, and, in 1864 Brownlow actually placed Johnson's name in nomination for vice-president. Their political feud resumed on Johnson's ascent to the White House. Brownlow, now governor, reinstituted martial law in 10 counties due to civil unrest. Although the two never met as political opponents for the same office, they played an electoral hopscotch between the state's highest offices, with Brownlow succeeding Johnson as governor in 1865 and Johnson succeeding Brownlow as Senator in 1875.

By 1887, under a banner proclaiming "The New South," national magazines like *Harper's Weekly* featured Tennessee as a Southern success story, bringing itself into line with the new paradigms resulting from the late war. Education was an important part of this effort, and schools became an early target of reactionary forces, some even temporarily shut down and their teachers run off by outlaw organizations like the Ku Klux Klan.

The media was less kind in 1925, when Tennessee became the object of world ridicule in the prosecution of school teacher John Scopes, who had broken state law by teaching Darwin's theory of evolution in the classroom. Legendary giant of jurisprudence Clarence Darrow and three-time presidential loser William Jennings Bryan squared off in the sweltering Dayton courtroom. Bryan won a Pyrrhic victory with the court's verdict of guilt against the evolutionist Scopes, but died within a few days of the trial's conclusion.

In a region noted for its eccentric political spectacles,

where the saying "politics makes strange bedfellows" is well understood, there has been little to equal the so-called "War of the Roses" gubernatorial campaign of 1886. The candidates, brothers Bob (D) and Alf (R) Taylor, literally had been childhood bedfellows growing up together in Carter County.

Southern political observer V. O. Key once wrote that in Tennessee there was not a one-party system—as in most other Southern states—but "two one-party systems." A fact of political life in Tennessee until recent times, the Democratic party's lock on the governorship and Republican control of local elections in the eastern part of the state were a legacy of Reconstruction perpetuated in this century by Memphis Mayor E.H. "Boss" Crump's brand of big-city machine politics translated to the state level. These spheres of influence remained largely intact until Senator Estes Kefauver broke Crump's control of the Democrats in 1948. In 1952, Tennessee voted Republican (for Gen. Dwight D. Eisenhower) in a presidential election—an early indication of a crack in the Democrats' "Solid South." That milestone was followed in the late 60s and early 70s by the realigning elections of

Senator Howard Baker—of Watergate Hearings fame—
and Governor Winfield Dunn, both Republicans. Since
1970, the two parties have achieved something close to
parity. Still, even this balance is skewed from time to time,
as in 1974-78 when Democrats appeared to misstep with
the election of controversial Governor Ray Blanton, only
to bounce back eight years later with popular two-termer
Ned Ray McWherter. In 1994, the equilibrium was upset
once again when political newcomers Fred Thompson and
Bill Frist, riding a national wave of anti-incumbent ill will,
took both of Tennessee's U.S. Senate seats from the
Democrats, including that formerly held by Vice-
President Al Gore Jr.

Transcending partisan politics and truly visionary in
its scope, the Tennessee Valley Authority has undoubtedly had the greatest impact on the state's landscape—political, economic, social or otherwise. The Great Depression
of the 1930s devastated the South more than any other
region of the country. Tennessee was especially hard hit
and would play a pivotal role in the region's recovery.
Created by the federal government in 1933, the Tennessee
Valley Authority was the crowning achievement of the

Progressive spirit in American politics. In the most ambitious construction effort undertaken since the Egyptian pyramids, 16 dams were built along the Tennessee River between 1933 and 1945, realizing Nebraska Senator George Norris' vision of "developing [the Tennessee River] systematically, as one great enterprise, to bring about the maximum control of navigation, of flood control and of the development of electricity."

In a short span of years, the TVA transformed Tennessee, changing lives with an impact unequalled by any event in its history except the Civil War. The immediate results were a skilled work force, cheap power, better schools—in short, all the necessary prerequisites for attracting industry and promoting economic development.

EX PRESIDENT & MRS JAS. K. POLK.
RESIDENCE NASHVILLE, TENNESSEE

President James K. Polk and Mrs. Polk (1795-1849)
A former speaker of the House of Representatives and
Tennessee governor, Polk was elected president over Henry
Clay in 1844. Due to his firm policies regarding the annexa-
tion of Texas and the Oregon boundary dispute with Britain,
many historians consider him to be the most effective one-term
chief executive in the nation's history

These sterling people from the Apppalachian region a half century ago rendered to this country an invaluable service. Without them this Union would have been divided. But for them the cause of secession would have inevitably succeeded.

Thomas Nelson Page on East Tennesseans' contribution to the Union victory in the Civil War

The administration [of occupied Tennessee] was conducted according to the will and pleasure of the governor, which was the supreme law.

Jefferson Davis on Andrew Johnson's absolute power as military governor of Tennessee, 1862-65

It is not expected that the enemies of the United States will propose to vote, nor is it intended that they be permitted to vote, or hold office.

Governor Andrew Johnson, disenfranchising the Tennessee secessionists, 1864

$\mathscr{N}$o man has the right to judge Andrew Johnson in any respect, who has not suffered as much and done as much as he for the nation's sake.
President Abraham Lincoln, 1864

$\mathscr{T}$ailor! Plebeian! Lowborn!
various epithets used to describe Andrew Johnson by his political enemies

$\mathscr{I}$ am going to tell the truth here today, and that is I am a plebian—and I thank God for it!
Vice-President Andrew Johnson, Inaugural Day, 1865

$\mathscr{D}$on't you bother about Andy Johnson's drinking. He made a bad slip the other day, but I have known Andy a great many years, and he ain't no drunkard.
Abraham Lincoln, 1865. Johnson was widely reported to have been drunk when he took the oath of office on Inaugural Day. Actually, he was suffering from a fever and had quaffed brandy from a friend's flask as a home remedy

No impartial reader can examine the record without feeling that the president was impeached for one series of misdemeanors and tried for another series.
James G. Blaine on President Johnson's impeachment, 1868

I have battled against Andrew Johnson perserveringly, systematically, and terribly for a quarter of a century.
William G. "Parson" Brownlow

I expect to stand by this Union, and battle to sustain it, though Whiggery and Democracy, Slavery and Abolitionism, Southern rights and Northern wrongs are all blown to the devil!
William G. "Parson" Brownlow, Reconstruction governor of Tennessee, 1865-69

Abolish the Loyal League and the Ku Klux Klan; let us come together and stand together.
Nathan Bedford Forrest, the first Grand Wizard of the original KKK, calling for an end to civil unrest, 1868

*W*e were born on the same soil, breathe the same air, live on the same land, and why should we not be brothers and sisters?

Nathan Bedford Forrest, addressing the black community of Memphis at the City Fair Grounds, July 5, 1875

I am dictating an obituary notice of the death of Andrew Johnson. When I was elected to the Senate, it was objected to me that I would not live out my term, and here I am, with a good appetite and a clear conscience, writing the obituary of my successor.

William G. Brownlow, 1875. Although questions concerning his advancing age and failing health were raised by political opponents, Brownlow served one term as U.S. senator before he was succeeded by former President Andrew Johnson, who died soon thereafter

William G. Brownlow (1805-1877)
A former newspaper editor and Methodist circuit rider,
Brownlow was a staunch supporter of the Union during the
Civil War. Briefly jailed by the Confederates, Brownlow fled
the state. He became Reconstruction governor in 1865
and later U.S. senator

What is it but the increase and diffusion of knowledge that has given us our arts, our sciences, our manufactures, our comforts, our luxuries, our civilization? And from what did this increase of knowledge arise but from observing the operations and studying the laws of nature?

Matthew Fontaine Maury, who oversaw the laying of the first trans-Atlantic telegraphic cable from North America to Europe, 1868

Education is the cheapest defense of nations. No police expenditures are so effective as those of an educational nature. School teachers and school books cost much less than jails and penitentiaries and criminal courts.

Dr. John Berrien Lindsley, public education pioneer, addressing the State Teachers Association meeting in Chattanooga, 1869

*T*he people of Tennessee will count him a public benefactor who will direct the popular energies to useful pursuits to diversification of labor, to the encouragement of immigration, the opening of mines, the improvement of agriculture, the erection of schoolhouses, and especially ... the utter abolition of all local jealousies and animosities, and for the encouragement and perpetuation of a spirit of brotherhood among the people of all the states of the Union.

Governor James D. Porter, inaugural address, 1874

*W*e had dreamed together in the same trundle bed, and often kicked each other out. ... But now the dreams of our manhood clashed. With flushed cheeks and throbbing hearts, we eagerly entered the field, his shield bearing the red rose, mine the white. The multitude gathered, a white rose on every Democratic bosom and a red rose on every Republican breast.

Robert L. Taylor, describing the "War of the Roses" campaign of 1888, when he and his brother Alfred ran against each other for governor of Tennessee. Robert won this contest, but Alfred was elected in 1920 and served until 1923

*L*ook yonder at those flashing domes and glittering spires. Look what Southern brains and Southern hands have wrought. See the victories of peace we have won, all represented within the white columns of our great industrial exposition, and you will receive an inspiration of the Old South, and you will catch glimpses of her future glory.

Governor Robert Love Taylor speaking at the Tennessee Centennial Exposition on the New South industrial spirit, 1897

I see no reason why our government should not build and maintain a national highway system, running to all parts of the country. It would be far better than spending the money for battleships, large standing armies and profligate pensions.

Kenneth D. McKellar, U.S. Congressman from Memphis, 1911

*H*urrah and vote for suffrage! Don't keep them in doubt. Don't forget to be a good boy and help Mrs. Catt put the 'rat' in ratification.

Letter to Representative Harry Burn from his mother in Niota. Mr. Burn cast the deciding vote that led to Tennessee's ratification of the 19th Amendment, which gave women the right to vote in all elections

Robert Love Taylor (1850-1912)
Taylor, a Democrat, defeated his brother in the famous "War of
the Roses" election of 1886, served three terms as governor,
and, at the time of his death, was a U.S. senator

That it shall be unlawful for any teacher in any of the Universities, Normals and all other public schools of the State to teach any theory that denies the story of the Divine Creation of man as taught in the Bible, and to teach instead that man has descended from a lower order of animals.

the law Dayton schoolteacher John Scopes, who was brought to trial and fined $100 for violated by his actions, 1925

The people of Tennessee have a right to protect the Bible as they understand it. They are not compelled to consider the interpretations placed upon it by people of other states, whether Christians or scientists, or both.

William Jennings Bryan, Scopes trial

He was sincere in his beliefs. The Dayton trial was his death blow.

Rev. Charles Francis Potter on William Jennings Bryan, who died at Dayton within a week after the conclusion of the Scopes trial, July 26, 1925

Scopes Trial
In the sweltering July of 1925, after 11 days of vigorous, near-violent debate between Clarence Darrow and William Jennings Bryan, schoolteacher John Scopes was found guilty of violating Tennessee's anti-evolution law and fined $100.
More significant than the actual verdict, however, was the fact that the case was tried in the world press, where the state was subjected to routine humiliation

The Tennessee itself is now a wild, untamed stream. It is one of the greatest rivers of the United States. ... All along the valley, the chief interest is farming, but the farmers are mostly poor. By careless treatment of the land, the forests have been cut off, the steep slopes have been plowed, and much of the good soil has been washed away. On the soil which is left, the people continue their wasteful ways. They work hard but grow poorer along with the land. They have few modern conveniences, but struggle along in a life of drudgery. Give the government permission to show what it can teach these unfortunate Americans.

President Franklin D. Roosevelt asking Congress to create the Tennessee Valley Authority, 1933

I look forward with keen anticipation to fishing and duck hunting on the placid surface of that great lake that will result from the construction of Norris Dam.

J. Will Taylor, Republican congressman 1933

*W*e wanted those dams to have the honest beauty of a fine tool, for TVA was a tool to do a job for men in a democracy.
David E. Lilienthal, chairman, Tennessee Valley Authority

*T*he East Tennessee Republicans were about to receive from the Democratic pork barrel more generous hunks of favor than any Republican dispenser, from Lincoln on down, had been able to offer.
Donald Davidson, on TVA

*N*ever put a sponge on the end of a hammer if you expect to drive a nail.
E.H. "Boss" Crump, mayor of Memphis

*Y*ou have accepted this [a seat in Congress] for 14 years as a gift from him. Now he wants it.
Representative Gordon Browning to his colleague Hubert Fisher, on the latter's forced retirement at the insistence of "Boss" Crump, 1930. Fisher was old and hard of hearing, and Crump had decided to go to Washington himself

E.H. Crump

Within a dozen years after arriving in Memphis penniless, Edward Hull Crump rose to become a dominate force in Memphis and Tennessee politics, officially and unofficially, for over 45 years.

In the art galleries of Paris, there are 27 pictures of Judas Iscariot—none look alike but all resemble Gordon Browning.
"Boss" Crump, 1938

I may be a pet coon, but I'm not Mr. Crump's pet coon.
Estes Kefauver, whose successful campaign for the U.S. Senate in 1948 broke "Boss" Crump's hold over state politics. When Crump compared Kefauver to "a pet coon that puts its foot in your bureau drawer, and when you catch him, looks the other way and hopes he will deceive any onlookers as to where his foot is and what it is into," Kefauver put on a coonskin cap and with defiance hurled the words back into Crump's face

You can ride but you cannot drive.
Gordon Browning to "Boss" Crump, after winning his first term as governor, 1936

*T*o many Americans, sick of the corruption they hear about so often. ... Mr. Kefauver stands as a courageous fighter for clean government.
The New York Times on Senator Estes Kefauver, who ran as Adlai Stevenson's vice-presidential nominee, 1956

*I*f a man wants to buy an automobile, get married or run for political office, he will do just that regardless of advice.
Frank G. Clement, 1952. Clement would be elected governor three times. In years when he was constitutionally prohibited from succeeding himself, his campaign manager and protegé Buford Ellington served as governor

*A*merica is never going to find security in oppression. America is going to find strength only in free men who have the right to speak and think as they wish.
Senator Estes Kefauver, 1950

This is a new experience for me. All my life I've gotten almost everything I asked for, it seems like. I hope the people will unite behind me for the next two years.

Governor Frank G. Clement, after his attempt to be elected U.S. senator while still a sitting governor was rejected by Tennessee voters. A Senate vacancy occurred when Estes Kefauver died suddenly in 1963. Clement was defeated in the Democratic primary by Congressman Ross Bass, 1964. In 1966, Clement would take his party's nomination away from Bass, only to lose to Howard Baker Jr. in the general election

There was a kind of satisfaction in the last moments of my political career. After a battle in which I had fought with every ounce of my being for what I sincerely believed to be right, I closed by saying, "The causes for which we fought are not dead. The truth shall rise again."

Sen. Albert Gore Sr., considered so liberal by his opponents in Tennessee that he was tagged "The Third Senator from Massachusetts." He lost his seat to Republican Bill Brock in 1970

It is not a happy day for me.

Lamar Alexander, upon being sworn in as governor three days early to prevent Governor Ray Blanton, under investigation for abuse of executive power, from pardoning any more convicts, 1979

This is not another Watergate.

former U.S. Senator Howard Baker, commenting on the Iran-Contra scandal, which broke late in 1986 and threatened the effectiveness of the Reagan presidency. After a White House reshuffling, Baker returned to public life as Reagan's chief-of-staff, where his presence as a venerable elder statesman did much to restore public confidence in the administration

Ann Dallas Dudley (1876-1955)
Pictured with her children. Dudley played a leading role in the Women's Suffrage Movement. She was the first president of the Tennessee Equal Suffrage League and an officer of the National American Woman Suffrage League

The revolutionary new means to store and retrieve information, as well as the new kinds of rapid transportation and instant communication, have enormous implications for the kind of world we will live in tomorrow.

U.S. Senator Albert Gore Jr., championing "clean" technology, 1986. As vice-president, Gore has focused national attention on America's high-tech possibilities

No one should think that government alone is the author of our progress in this state. This is the home of Davy Crockett, Sequoyah, Nancy Ward, Alvin York, W.C. Handy, Alex Haley, Wilma Rudolph, Elvis and Minnie and Dinah and countless other Tennesseans who have enriched and inspired the lives of millions throughout the nation and the world.

Governor Don Sundquist, inaugural address, January 21, 1995

Chapter Five

Uncommon Resilience:
The Contributions of African-Americans

We hope that this war may serve to lift the scales from the eyes of prejudice-ridden America, and that the part we take in this fight will accomplish the required result, making the democracy of which we so much boast be a reality and not a mockery.
James A. Jones, Presiding Elder, A.M.E. Church, Nashville, on World War I

*I*n his novel Invisible Man, author Ralph Ellison uses a paint factory as a metaphor to emphasize the unsung and obscured contributions of African-Americans to U.S. history. Initially, the paint base is black, but the end product is white. The paint factory is a profound, effective image, and one that finds an immediate analogue in Tennessee history. In the rush to tell the sweeping story of Tennessee's settlement, the fact that the first settlers who came down the Nolichucky River in the 1760s had

African slaves with them is too often omitted. Moreover, the Overmountain men who fought the British at King's Mountain in 1780 were accompanied by black servants who joined in the fray and participated admirably in combat.

In 1818, the Jackson Purchase opened West Tennessee to white settlement. The fertile land of this last Grand Division was most akin to the Deep South cotton states; thus, plantation agriculture and its concomitant slave system influenced West Tennessee strongly, allowing a small but wealthy minority of planters to wield enormous political power. In the 1860 census, the slave population of West Tennessee was estimated at 40 percent of the total, and in a few counties exceeded 50 percent. In Middle Tennessee slaves constituted 25 percent of the population. Comparatively few slaves, only 8 percent, lived in the mountains of East Tennessee. However, the same 1860 census reported nearly 7,500 free blacks residing in Tennessee, an anomaly inconceivable in other slave states.

Apart from the intrinsically evil, corrupting character of the South's "peculiar institution," and the inevitable abuses that arose from one group's lawful use of "unrestrained personal power" to subjugate another, the most criminal aspect of slavery and the "Jim Crow" laws that followed it was the denial of economic opportunity to blacks in a free labor market. Indeed, it has only been in recent times that officially sanctioned, race-based barriers have been removed.

After the modest inroads made by black legislators during the Reconstruction era were quickly paved over by poll taxes, secret ballots, violence and the U.S. Supreme Court's 1896 affirmation of Plessy vs. Ferguson, blacks were discouraged from even voting, much less holding public office. Not until 1964 was the next African-American, Memphis attorney and NAACP counsel A.W. Willis Jr., elected to the General Assembly. It was 1974 before Harold Ford, also of Memphis, became the first black Tennessean to be seated in Congress.

These overdue victories were not without great cost. Beginning in February 1960, students of predominantly black colleges staged sit-ins at segregated lunch counters in the state's major cities. By 1968, desegregation was being implemented, but economic opportunity lagged behind, and Memphis sanitation workers, most of whom were black, went on strike. The strike turned from a labor dispute into a civil-rights battle when the city refused to meet the workers' demands. Dr. Martin Luther King was brought to Memphis on a fateful mission to organize the striking workers. Tragically, on April 4, 1968, King was martyred by a sniper's bullet as he stood on the balcony of the Lorraine Motel. Although neither Dr. King nor his assassin were Tennesseans, the murder focused national attention on racial problems in Memphis and was seen as an unparalleled disgrace to both the city and the state.

In 1977, unprecedented numbers of Americans tuned in to a weeklong television adaptation (history's first "mini-series") of Alex Haley's prize-winning generational novel Roots. With his story of the black family's plight in America, Haley, who spent his childhood in Henning, Tennessee, struck a chord with the nation that transcended racial lines. Roots did more in that one week to broaden understanding between the races than any other single media event in history. Indeed, while earlier media depictions of the South will no doubt endure as cultural relics, critics agree that Haley's images of plantation life are the most realistic, important ones. As such, they supplant the regressive stereotypes perpetuated by films such as *Birth of a Nation* or *Gone With the Wind*.

The blood of white and black men has flowed freely together for the great cause which is to give freedom. ... Colored troops exhibited courage and steadiness that challenged the admiration of all who witnessed their charge.

General George Thomas commenting on the bravery of African-American soldiers at the Battle of Nashville, 1864

Alex Haley
A Pulitzer prize-winning author best known for
his work, Roots, Haley's first work, *The
Autobiography of Malcolm X*, chronicled the life of
the civil rights leader.

I have not a good war record. The first reason I had for not going into the army was that they told me it was a white man's fight, and they did not want Negroes. The first Negroes were put into the war as slaves, and I did not go in. Another thing, they did not allow promotion among the colored soldiers, and I did not want any fighting on that plan. Another reason is that there was killing going on, and I was afraid I might get shot.

Ed Shaw, Reconstruction politician and first black Tennessean to run for Congress, in the Daily Memphis Avalanche, 1870

It is well-known that in one of Abraham Lincoln's proclamations he said that if the rebels would lay down their arms, he would give them back their fugitive slaves. It was God who liberated the slaves, and it was only a war measure; an incident of the war.

Ed Shaw

When the Irishman or the German comes to this country, his children are admitted to the schools the very day after they land, while the children of us native Americans are not allowed to enter them, but are set apart, tabooed, ostracized.

Ed Shaw, 1872

Four hundred thousand black citizens are citizens de jure, but are aliens de facto and entitled to no rights which the railroads, hotels and theatres are bound to respect.

Thomas A. Sykes, Thomas F. Cassels, Isaac F. Norris and John W. Boyd, four black legislators elected in 1880, protesting a state segregation law of 1875 that barred blacks from public facilities and relegated them to second-class accommodations

I had hoped such great things from my suit for my people generally. I have firmly believed all along that the law was on our side and would, when we appealed to it, give us justice. I feel shorn of that belief and utterly discouraged.

Ida B. Wells, public school teacher, journalist and advocate for racial justice and women's rights, 1887. After a train conductor forced her out of the first-class section near Woodstock, a small town just outside Memphis, Wells became the first African-American to challenge the 1883 nullification of the Civil Rights Bill passed during Reconstruction. She successfully sued the Chesapeake & Ohio Railway, only to have her victory voided by a higher court

*M*ister Crump don't 'low no easy riders here
Mister Crump don't 'low no easy riders here
I don't care what Mr. Crump don't 'low
I'm gonna barrelhouse anyhow
Mr. Crump can go catch hisself some air

W.C. Handy in Crump mayoral election theme song (later to become "Memphis Blues"), 1909. Oddly, while Crump ran on a clean-up-government platform, most blacks favored a "wide-open town"

*N*egroes do not vote in Memphis; they are voted.
common saying in Shelby County during the Crump era

*A*lthough I have been spared many of the harsher manifestations of civil wrongs, I rejoice in the victory of black Americans over racism and bigotry. It is not yet a complete victory, but it is substantial and continuing. I am by nature an optimist about the future.
William Oscar Smith, founder of W.O. Smith Nashville School of Music

*W*e hold that our devotion to our country, to its flag, and to its government, entitles us to all that it gives other citizens. Whenever called upon, we cheerfully and patriotically buy bonds, subscribe to the Red Cross, render service in the furrows or in the trenches, shed blood or give up our lives for the defense of our country. ... If these qualities do not entitle us to a fair chance in the race for life, pray tell us what any set of people ever has or can do to win that chance.
James Carroll Napier, Nashville businessman and president of the National Negro Business League, 1917

Any day you go to the corner of 35th and State Streets in Chicago, you will see someone from Knoxville if you wait long enough.
a common saying among East Tennessee African-Americans

Beale Street, owned largely by the Jews, policed by the Whites, and enjoyed by the Negroes, is the Main Street of Negro America.
George Washington Lee, 1934

The glory that was Greece, the grandeur that was Rome, the "blues" that is Beale.
George Washington Lee, 1934

There is a saying about people who have achieved a position. Anytime you see a turtle atop a fence post, you know it had some help.
Alex Haley, author, 1992

In writing about segregation, one has the feeling that he is discussing a problem that should have been solved a century ago. Indeed, this stands out as particularly true in our case, since, as Americans, we feel that we have a position of leadership in the Western world, and world leadership and segregation are simply not compatible in the 20th century. I think it should be frankly stated that we are really dealing with an anachronism.

Mortimer May, Nashville businessman, 1959

Ryman Auditorium, Nashville
Roy Acuff once remarked, "I had never seen a country music show until I put one on." For decades, performing at the Ryman, home of the Grand Ole Opry, marked the summit of success in country music

CHAPTER SIX
LARGER THAN LIFE

If I had a thousand lives, I would lose them all here before I would betray my friends or the confidence of my informer.
LAST WORDS OF 19-YEAR-OLD SAM DAVIS, CONFEDERATE STATES OF AMERICA, BEFORE HIS EXECUTION BY THE UNION ARMY FOR ESPIONAGE

*S*eemingly in every field of human endeavor, Tennessee has produced sons and daughters who have attained legendary status. James Hampton Kirkland, a former chancellor of Vanderbilt University, said "Great men may not be all of history, but they make possible all the rest. Abstract ideas do not bear a nation onward or upward. It is only when these have been incarnated into a great life that they may be grasped and assimilated. Happy the country that has produced a hero."

Often the word "hero" is narrowly applied only to great political leaders or intrepid warriors, and, as is evident from preceding chapters, Tennessee has certainly had its share of these. But the word deserves a broader definition. In early frontier days, ordinary "heroes" could be found living up the forks of any creek—heroes simply by virtue of their willingness to leave the security of civilization for the privations of the unknown and establish there a foundation for future generations to build upon. Yet even among such a distinctive group of trailblazers, men like Daniel Boone and Andrew Jackson stand apart from the rest. Other heroes, like Confederate spy Sam Davis or locomotive engineer Casey Jones, made the ultimate sacrifice and gave their own lives for others. No doubt, they would say they were only doing their duty. During World War I, another Tennessean, Sgt. Alvin York followed his sense of duty and reconsidered his application for reclassification as a "conscientious objector," a decision that led to his single-handed capture of 132 German soldiers at the Battle of the Argonne Forest, a feat he characteristically downplayed. Other Tennessee natives, like aviatrix Cornelia Fort and author Richard

Halliburton, were fearless, lone adventurers whose exploits vicariously thrilled ordinary folk around the country. With such a rich legacy of object lessons to draw upon, the deeds of these heroes and others like them will always challenge and inspire successive generations of Tennesseans to ever-grander accomplishments.

All true! Every word true! Not a lie in it!
Daniel Boone, late in life, defending John Filson's record of his autobiography, which established the Boone legend

*I*d rather fight the British again than have any more dealings with that torment.
Andrew Jackson, after spending the night at the home of John Bell. During Jackson's visit, the Bell Witch sang, swore, threw dishes, overturned furniture and snatched the bedclothes from all the beds

*I*f our people think I am making a fool of myself, you may tell them that what I am doing will not make fools of them.
Sequoyah, inventor of the Cherokee syllabary, whose scholarly labors were misunderstood until the alphabet's completion, 1826. At one point, Sequoyah's disgusted, impatient wife even burned his materials

*T*o establish a community in which Negro slaves should be educated and upraised to a level with the Whites, and thus prepared for freedom; and to set an example, which, if carried out, would eventually abolish slavery.
Frances Wright, founder of the utopian colony of Nashoba, a noble but failed experiment, c. 1826

Annie Cook, the woman who, after a long life of shame, ventured all she had of life and property for the sick, died September 11th of yellow fever, which she contracted by nursing her patients.

obituary of Annie Cook, who ran a brothel at The Mansion House, #34 Gayoso Street, Memphis, 1878

Bose Lashley, an M&O brakeman, looked up from his plate when the lanky Jones came in to be seated. "What's your name son?" he asked. "John Luther Jones," the youngster replied. "Where are you from?" asked Lashley. "Cayce, Kentucky," said Jones. "Well, sit down Cayce and make yourself at home," Lashley replied.

story of how Casey Jones received his nickname at his boarding house in Jackson, Tennessee

*J*ump, Sim, jump!

Casey Jones last words to his fireman Sim Webb, April 30, 1900. Casey stayed with his engine, applying the brakes to lessen the impact of the impending collision with the last four cars of Train No. 83, which were stalled on the mainline. His selfless act cost Jones his life but saved his passengers

I got a boat load and put 'em on the bank. My boat holds 12 but I don't know how many I had. It wasn't no time for counting heads.

Tom Lee, who could not swim, recounting how he saved 32 lives when the steamboat M.E. Norman sank about 20 miles below Memphis, 1925. Lee was a black man who, after his heroic deed, was held up as a model citizen of his race by Memphis' white community. Ironically, they named a segregated park in his honor

*W*hen you are an old man, I want you to remember that your old teacher said, "Don't ever be a spectator; take a hand in the game!"

William R. "Sawney" Webb, founder of Webb School at Bellbuckle, U.S. senator and mentor to dozens of Webb's distinguished alumni

There are those in this country today who ask me and other veterans of World War Number One, "What did it get you?" The thing they forget is that liberty and freedom and democracy are so very precious that you do not fight to win them once and stop. You do not do that. Liberty and Freedom and Democracy are prizes awarded only to those peoples who fight to win them and then keep fighting eternally to hold them.
Sgt. Alvin York

I reside where there is a good fight. I don't believe in women's rights, not in men's rights. I believe in human rights.
Mary Harris "Mother" Jones, labor organizer

*H*owever difficult the road may be, there is no hope of turning victory into enduring peace unless the real interests of this country, the British Commonwealth, the Soviet Union and China are harmonized, and unless they agree and act together. This is the solid framework upon which all future policy and international organization must be built.

Cordell Hull, FDR's secretary of state and former U.S. Senator from Tennessee, laying the groundwork for the United Nations, 1944

*H*e flew too near the sun.

inscription on a monument located on the campus of Rhodes College, to Memphis native Richard Halliburton. Halliburton, an author and adventurer who won a huge popular following for his books about exotic climes, perished while attempting to cross the Pacific Ocean in a Chinese junk in 1939

*G*eneral Neyland doesn't throw the ball much, but when he does he hurts you.

Bear Bryant, legendary Alabama football coach, who, in eight tries, failed to beat Gen. Robert Neyland's Tennessee Volunteers. Neyland retired after the 1952 season

*W*hat I like about being back in Clarksville, everybody here just treats me as "Skeeter," and I feel so at ease here. Now that I'm back, I feel that Tennessee is just the place for me.

Wilma Rudolph, after winning three gold medals in track and field at the 1960 Olympics

I love flying because it taught me utter self-sufficiency, the ability to remove oneself beyond the keep of anyone at all, and, in so doing, it taught me what was of value and what was not. If I die violently, who can say it was "before my time?" I should have dearly loved to have a husband and children. My talents in that line would have been pretty good, but if that is to be, I want no one to grieve for me.

Cornelia Fort, aviator, in a letter to her mother, 1942

Tennessee State Capitol Building
Designed by William Strickland, one of the leading architects
of the day, the Tennessee State Capitol building has housed
the legislative proceedings of the General Assembly since
1853, except for a brief hiatus during the Civil War.
Its construction took 14 years

CHAPTER SEVEN
LIFEWAYS OF YESTERYEAR

There is a certainty of profitable returns from
whatever is put into the soil.
T. F. PECK, AGRICULTURE COMMISSIONER, 1922

*I*n 1960, Tennessee crossed a significant demographic threshold. For the first time, a census indicated that there were more Tennesseans residing in urban areas than rural. The body politic's shift from country to city—a phenomenon accompanied by a near doubling in the state's population—was the culmination of an extended migration pattern traceable to the final decades of the 1800s. As widespread poverty and the decline of the traditional family farm contributed to a rural exodus of all but the most self-reliant, thousands of blacks and whites flocked to the state's urban centers. Despite some setbacks such as the Yellow Fever epidemic of 1878, which hit Memphis and Chattanooga especially hard, the cities prospered thanks to industry.

However, one did not have to be a city dweller to experience the extreme changes in everyday life that occurred literally within a single generation. The coming of the Tennessee Valley Authority and rural electrification in the 1930s made "King Kilowatt" equally accessible to the small towns and communities that still remain the backbone of the state. Indeed, it seems impossible to over-estimate the impact of TVA on the daily lives of Tennesseans, as well as to those citizens of surrounding states, who are served by the agency. As one Chattanooga citizen, describing the 60 year effect of TVA on his area observed, the agency has made "the difference between daylight and dark."

Of course, while electricity did improve the quality of human life, it was not within its power to make up for human shortcomings, and, undoubtedly, some of the quotes in this chapter will bring to mind the old adage,

"The more things change the more they remain the same." Tennesseans have always been concerned with issues that affect the quality of their lives, from violent crime to corruption in high places. While today's headlines may seem full of despair, it is important to realize that the past was never a perfect world either. Fortunately, there continues to be a clear majority of wise and good-intentioned people in the state doing their utmost to make Tennessee a better place for all its diverse people.

Agriculture is the basis upon which society and all that is valuable to men rests; take away the ground work, and everything falls.

John Overton

Tennessee Centennial and International Exposition, c. 1897
General view of the grounds. To the left can be seen the rising pinnacle of the Egyptian pyramid that housed the Memphis/Shelby County exhibit. Further to the left and in the distance is the
State Capitol Building

The farmers of our state are more prosperous than at any time for 30 or 40 years past.
John Thompson, agriculture commissioner, 1908

It ain't anything to see a man come in and trade in a tractor and a three-year-old Buick and $100 down on a span of hard-tail mules.
Will Rogers, on Mule Day in Columbia, 1930s

Then came the merchant, and we all got into debt; the lawyer and we all got law; the doctor, and we all got sick; the preacher, and we all got religion.
Christian Carriger, member of the pre-Civil War legislature, 1868

It seems that the devil left hell on a vacation, stopped over at Memphis, sat down on Beale Street and rewrote the Ten Commandments leaving the NOT out of each commandment.
a black minister to his congregation, c. 1920

*I*f any student shall be guilty of fighting, striking, quarrelling, challenging, turbulent words or behavior, wearing women's apparel, fraud, lying, defamation or any such like crime, he shall be punished by firm admonition or other College punishments suited to the nature and demerit of the crime.

excerpted from the rules of East Tennessee University, Knoxville, 1821

*E*verybody in this community who wishes to do so, carries a pistol. The enforcement of the law against pistol-carrying in this country is such a force that nobody hesitates to go armed.

Memphis Commercial Appeal, 1901

*K*illing is now the most thriving industry in this part of the country.

Memphis Commercial Appeal, 1909

There was a smell about court days—manure, sweat, watermelons, horses, mules and tobacco! The aroma of a circus—an odor of life! Court days, somehow, always seemed the hottest of the summer.

Evelyn Scott in Background in Tennessee, *describing Clarksville on the day when the county court sat, 1937*

Litigation is an evil incident to our nature.

Judge John Overton

That lawsuit may be settled at the courthouse, but it's not been settled up the holler yet.

old East Tennessee saying

The country newspaper has been the unfaltering, the faithful and conservative counselor of the people. It turns the minds of men to the love of country, of home and of the fireside, and arrests the decay of patriotism, that freedom may live with posterity.

U.S. Representative John A. Moon (D-Tennessee), 1898. Congressman Moon has been called the "father of the parcel post," having helped establish it as chairman of the House Post Office Committee

The hospital is awful handy to the graveyard.

an example of the dark humor published during the 1877 yellow fever epidemic by Chattanooga Times owner Adolph Ochs. Later in his career Ochs would buy The New York Times and coin the slogan "ALL THE NEWS THAT'S FIT TO PRINT"

The engine stood impatiently, and its metallic parts scattered the smell of oily steam and cinders. The very cries of welcome and farewell, the loading and unloading, told you it would not tarry. And out of the steam the 'All aboard,' sharp and vaporous. But already the wheels were hissing; they spun; slowly and invincibly they caught the rails, turning, turning out of sight the train on its way to unknown parts.

Andrew Lytle, man-of-letters

Take of London fog 30 parts; malaria 10 parts; gas leaks 20 parts; dewdrops gathered in a brick yard at sunrise; odor of honeysuckle 15 parts. Mix.

O. Henry on the air quality of Nashville, 1909

I wonder why they gave it such a name of old renown, this dreary, dismal, muddy, melancholy town.

William H. Russell, British newspaperman, speaking of Memphis, 1862

*T*here were no sidewalks, and when it rained, the dirt street turned into a huge, four-block-square mud puddle. Hogs, wandering loose around town, considered it their private playground and congregated there to wallow away the day.

Minnie Pearl, Grand Ole Opry comedienne, describing Centerville as it appeared when her parents moved there, c. 1897

*T*hese people, I call 'em establishment bullies—the robber barons, the coal barons—came into the colony of Appalachia. Appalachia is a colony in the truest sense of the word. It has all the earmarks—the absentee landlords; nothing built of permanence. What has happened in other areas can show you what will happen to us when profit from the coal is gone. These entire valleys will be flooded for tourism and cheap power.

John Tiller, ex-coal miner

*T*ain't goin' to sell, but I ain't goin' to give you no trouble. I am just goin' to set here in my rocking chair and let the waters come up around me and drown me.

Old Aunt Rachel—in the annals of TVA, a legendary "holdout" who resisted offers to be compensated for her land, which was scheduled to be flooded

*Y*ou couldn't law electricity on me.

Bert Garner, modern hermit, using mountain idiom to express his preference for kerosene and disdain for the TVA way

*W*ith TVA as her kitchen maid, Mrs. Memphis will have more time for her educational and cultural activities.

Mrs. Merrill P. Hudson, Memphis civic and social leader, 1934

I know that the real heroes of our time are not governors and presidents but parents, farmers, teachers, ministers, athletes, soldiers, the people who make the cars we drive and the music we love, the people who care for those in need and never get—or expect—a bit of credit. ... And let us go forward together to make the undiscovered country that is our future a summerland of opportunity and purpose, safety and dignity and prosperity for every Tennessean.

Governor Don Sundquist, inaugural address, January 21, 1995

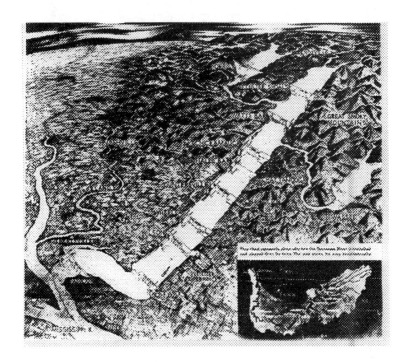

Tennessee Valley Authority

The Tennessee Valley Authority "conquered" the Tennessee River, which was, as Donald Davidson noted, "the product of engineering operations of such calculated daring that the imagination is daunted to find precedent for them."

Bedwell, Randall J. May I Quote You, General Lee?.
Memphis and Nashville: Guild Bindery Press, 1995.

Callahan, North. TVA: Bridge Over Troubled Waters.
South Brunswick, New Jersey: A.S. Barnes, 1980.

Connelly, Thomas Lawrence. Army of the Heartland:
The Army of Tennessee, 1861–1862. Baton Rouge:
Louisiana State University Press, 1967.

Corlew, Robert Ewing. Tennessee, A Short History.
Knoxville: University of Tennessee Press, 1990.

Davidson, Donald. The Tennessee: The Old River,
Frontier to Secession. Franklin: John S. Sanders.
Reprint of 1946 edition.

Doyle, Don. Nashville in the New South. Knoxville:
University of Tennessee Press, 1985.

Drake, Edwin L. The Annals of the Army of Tennessee.
Memphis: Guild Bindery Press, 1994. Reprint of 1904
edition.

Driver, Carl Samuel. John Sevier, Pioneer of the Old Southwest. Chapel Hill: University of North Carolina Press, 1932.

Dykeman, Wilma. Tennessee: A Bicentennial History. New York: Norton, 1975.

Folmsbee, Stanley J., Corlew, Robert E. and Mitchell, Enock. History of Tennessee. 2 volumes. New York: Lewis Historical Publishing, 1960.

Frome, Michael. Strangers in High Places: The Story of the Great Smoky Mountains. Knoxville: University of Tennessee Press, 1980.

Harkins, John. Metropolis of the American Nile: Memphis and Shelby County, An Illustrated History. Memphis: Guild Bindery Press, 1991.

Harper, Herbert L. ed. Houston and Crockett, Heroes of Tennessee and Texas. Nashville: Tennessee Historical Commission, 1986.

Hull, Cordell. The Memoirs of Cordell Hull. New York: Macmillan, 1948.

Jones, Billy M. ed. Heroes of Tennessee. Memphis: Memphis State University Press, 1979.

Lamon, Lester C. Blacks in Tennessee. Knoxville: Published in cooperation with the Tennessee Historical Commission [by] University of Tennessee Press, 1981.

Lee, Fred J. Casey Jones. Memphis: Guild Bindery Press, 1993. Reprint of 1940 edition.

Morton, John Watson. The Artillery of Nathan Bedford Forrest's Cavalry. Memphis: Guild Bindery Press, 1992.

Owsley, Frank L. Plain Folk of the Old South. Baton Rouge: Louisiana State University Press, 1949.

Putnam, Alligence Waldo. History of Middle Tennessee; or Life and Times of General James Robertson. Knoxville: University of Tennessee Press, 1971. Reprint of 1859 edition.

Remini, Robert V. Andrew Jackson and the Course of American Freedom, 1822-1832. New York: Harper and Row, 1981.

Stokely, Jim and Johnson Jeff D. ed. An Encyclopedia of East Tennessee. Oak Ridge, Tennessee: Children's Museum of Oak Ridge, 1981.

Temple, Oliver Perry. Notable Men of Tennessee, from 1833–1875, Their Times and Their Contemporaries. New York: The Cosmopolitan Press, 1912.

Whitman, Willson. God's Valley: People and Power along the Tennessee River. New York: Viking, 1939.

Williams, Samuel Cole. Beginnings of West Tennessee in the Land of the Chickasaws, 1541–1841. Johnson City, Tennessee: The Wautauga Press, 1930.

Williams, Samuel Cole. History of the Lost State of Franklin. Johnson City: The Wautauga Press, 1924.

Williams, Samuel Cole. Tennessee During the Revolutionary War. Johnson City: The Wautauga Press, 1944.

Wolfe, Charles K. Tennessee Strings: The Story of Country Music in Tennessee. Knoxville: University of Tennessee Press, 1977.

In the Shadow of the Wall by Carsten Kaaz. $22.95 hardcover. ISBN 1-55793-023-6. A compelling, true-life story about the author's childhood in the shadow of the Berlin Wall and his daring escape to freedom at age 20. "Riveting, true-life revelation. ... Kaaz succeeds in transforming that lone, death-defying experience into a universal tale of one man's search to triumph over evil."

— Memphis Business Journal

May I Quote You, General Lee? Volume I by Randall Bedwell. $9.95 flexicover. ISBN 1-55793-053-8. A collection of insightful and meaningful quotes from Confederate Generals Robert E. Lee, Nathan Bedford Forrest, Stonewall Jackson and others. A great gift for any Civil War buff. "The way of life they defended is gone forever but their names and words live forever." — the author

Daddies — An Endangered Species by Bill Haltom. $9.95 softcover. ISBN 1-55793-067-8. A humorous collection of articles on fatherhood compiled by this attorney/syndicated columnist/daddy. He comes from a long line of daddies, but he is worried about the species. "I believe the world needs daddies who stick around after conception, change diapers, help with homework and pay for the pediatric orthodontist's Mercedes." — the author

J. William Fulbright and His Time by Lee Riley Powell. $29.95 hardcover. ISBN 1-55793-060-0. Introduction by President Bill Clinton. The definitive biography of this great statesman. "A towering biography of a towering figure. ... An instant candidate for the Pulitzer Prize in biography." — Daniel Schorr

Unbroken Circle: A Quotable History of the Grand Old Opry by Randall Bedwell. $7.95 softcover. ISBN 1-55793-070-8. A celebration of America's longest running musical variety show, this entertaining volume features dozens of quotes from famous Opry stars throughout its seventy-one-year history, including many rare Opry photographs. Available August, 1996.

Country Music's Most Embarrassing Moments by Jim Dickerson. $7.95 softcover. ISBN 1-55793-059-7. This humorous book contains painfully true stories from country music's biggest stars about embarrassing moments that, for the first time, they have decided to share with their fans. They hold nothing back.

Money Memos: Maxims For Success From Maverick Entrepreneurs by Randall Bedwell. $7.95 softcover. Over 150 contemporary entrepreneurs share nuggets of wisdom in this book of inspirational quotations.

Money Memos: Putting Together A Portable Pension by Randall Bedwell $7.95 softcover. Contains indispensable advice on IRAs, 401Ks, Keoghs, SEPs and other retirement plans. Includes latest information on new federal legislation. Available July, 1996.

Money Memos: Financial Simplicity In A Complicated World by Randall Bedwell. $7.95 softcover. A concise guide to the intelligent use of money, from banking to budgeting, from spending to saving. Takes readers step-by-step through the essentials of achieving peace of mind through healthy financial living. Available July, 1996.

Credit Wisdom: A Guide to Better Financial Management by Randall Bedwell. $7.95 softcover. Demystifies debt with succinct information on every element of consumer borrowing and credit, including credit cards, auto and installment loans and mortgages. Available July, 1996.

Money Memos® titles are available by direct mail only or from financial institutions participating in the *Money Memos*® *Financial Education Series.* Ask a representative of your bank or financial institution about the *Money Memos*® series.

Please add $1.50 shipping and handling for the first book and $1.00 for each additional book.

Guild Bindery Press
P.O. Box 38099
Germantown, Tennessee 38183

You can also order books directly from our World Wide Webb page at: www.socomm.net//guild